Dream Big, Morena

Angelina Rodriguez

BookLeaf Publishing

India | USA | UK

Presentation by *BookLeaf Publishing*

Web: www.bookleafpub.com

E-mail: info@bookleafpub.com

ISBN: 9789360942960

First edition 2024

I dedicate this to every little brown girl, pushing further, just one day at a time. Stand in your power, trust your gut, use your voice and love your skin. You are so, so worthy.

ACKNOWLEDGEMENT

I wouldn't be writing this without my mom instilling in me that I can do anything. It wasn't in a traditional way, by any means, but I think that's why it stuck with me. I love you, mom. To my Tia, I know it hasn't always been easy, but thank you for always stepping up. It's never been unnoticed. To Rich, thank you for always coming through, even when you're a little grumpy and rough, I know you'll always be in my corner. I appreciate you. To my family, thank you for pushing my dreams forward with me. I learned things on my own for a long time and I'm grateful for where we are today. Not alone. To my siblings, I am so proud and thankful for our bond. We've been through a lot, and that's putting it simply. Just know, even when I'm the "not so fun" older sister, you'll never walk alone in this world. I love you all. To my dad, keep bettering yourself for you. Everything will continue to fall in place. I love you. To my best friends, Christina, Sabrina and Analisa, I can't thank you enough for all the love and support you've brought into my life. I don't even have to ask, you'll be there before I have the chance. I am forever grateful for you. Malinalcoatl and Ixochitemoc, thank you for always being there no matter what. Christina Amormino, you've been my shoulder so many times. Thank you for always cheering me on. Stephanie Anchondo, Ruby Rodriguez, Alexis Roman, Nicholas Aguilar, Zenaida Granados, Janelle Roman, Raylene and Marissa Mancilla, and of course all my CVM, I love and appreciate you always. Arabella, P, Joycelyn & Annavae, my loves, this world is too small for your greatness. Keep pushing, I will always root for you. Thank you for rooting just as hard for me for all these years. To my Nina Becca and my Nino Vince, the best godparents I could have ever been blessed with. Thank you for laying the example that showed me how to be a Nina. To my godchildren, just know now your Nina always has your back. To everyone I've ever organized with throughout all of our community work, thank you for being in space with me, and for continuing to fight until we see a world that is just. Lastly, Diana, my heart, my rock, my biggest fan, my confidant. I love you more than life itself, baby girl. I'm always in your corner, thank you for being you.

PREFACE

I was born brown in a time where brown babies, such as myself and my teen parents, were hyper-criminalized. 500 years of resilience was running through my veins and was meant to continue to become more resilient. More adaptable. An amazing blessing, with a lot of pressure. I feel journeys as brown people, as Chican@s, as indigenous people, are often overlooked. Media doesn't portray our stories correctly, history was intentionally written incorrectly. There's so much beauty and richness in our past, present and future. Who better than us to document the reflections of this beauty? The indigenous tradition of storytelling is in our DNA, passed onto us by our ancestors. These are a collection of my letters, stories if you will, to them, to myself, to you… To us. Ometeotl.

This Too Shall Pass
(Written April 2022)

You're worthy of everything good in life.

Your break was needed and the world isn't set up for you to be successful when taking these breaks to honor yourself. Yet you did and you still haven't figured things out, but things have still been lining up. You are so far from where you've been, even though you feel the same sometimes.

Even though you feel stagnant, your internal growth is there. Stand in that and accept that others will question it, that's fine. As long as you don't allow their uncertainty in you impact you questioning yourself.

You've always been the most analytical of yourself, so why think that's changed now? You've always strategically moved & ensured those moves held integrity, so why think that's changed now? You've practiced amnesty with so many people, and you deserve to give yourself that same energy. You are okay. You will always be okay.

Anything meant for you is already yours, what
isn't meant for you won't serve you just because
you keep pushing for it. Just as you will
continue to accept your blessings, accept the nos
and the not right nows, and know the difference
between the three. Love yourself.

Senter & Singleton
(Written March 2021)

Dear officer,

I would've got down on the ground without looking down a barrel.

I didn't move fast because I was startled by the door. The big sound scared me when you all busted into what's supposed to be my safe place.

I sleep here. I pray here. I play here. This is my home sir. My home might look different than yours, but my home is still a home sir. You treat it less than, like you treat me less than sir. You treat your power badly, as bad as you're treating me right now sir. Yet, you think it's okay for you to scare me into giving you a title like sir, sir.

You come into my home, point a gun in my face, manhandle my family. I am a 10 year old child. But you know that I'm a child, as you kick my crayons and step on my orange Nickelodeon VHS. My teacher said cops keep you safe, so why does my stomach hurt when I see you in my space? I don't ever feel safe. You make me feel shaky and weird. I want to tell you to leave but you told me to shut up. That's not nice to say to people, especially in their own houses you know?

It's also not nice for you to be throwing everything around. You're yelling at my mom and have her on the floor. This is her house too, you know?

You guys laugh and think it's funny, but I don't. I'm glad you're finally leaving. The court said our house is messy, but you made it messier, you know? Now I have to clean it all up. Even the things you broke, and you just get to leave.

What if I came to your house and did this? But I wouldn't so don't worry. My mom, the lady you're yelling at in front of me and all the other kids, you and your friends yelling at her. She taught me better. She taught me to be respectful. We don't need to demand respect with a gun, like you rude sir. Now, please get out of my house.

Sincerely,
The little brown girl from Senter and Singleton

Ueperi
(Written April 2021)

Dear Ueperi,

My love means vulnerability.
Not the fear of, but the push through.
My biggest fear still, but less so when I'm with
you.
It's working towards trust, instead of through
trust issues.
I am focused on building a foundation with you.
Hate conquered love, so many times, in so many
ways.
Anything, but love, is what I harbored most
days.
Years passed by, my love grew. I felt safe.
Because you gave me every reason to.

Until you didn't.

My love means I trust you, even when not fully
because my past gets in the way.
But I do trust you enough to heal together every
day.
I heal me, you heal you.

In tandem, we heal for anything that might come
our way.
Tu eres mi otro yo, mi dualidad.
Por Vida, Post Vida.
Regardless of our continued or discontinued ties.
Because when we focus on betterment, rather
than resentment, we center on building better
futures.
Whether together or apart.

Love always,
Your reciprocated but unreciprocated love

Morena
(Written April 2023)

I've always been brown.

Sometimes I'm golden brown when papa sol kisses my skin in the earlier days of the summer months. Sometimes my Apache indigeneity makes its presence known and my skin is more of a reddish-brown.

No matter what shade of brown I show up as, people always invite themselves to comment on my skin. I used to react with whatever emotion was heavy on my heart after hearing the tone of the comment. I'd hold back tears of hurt, shame and embarrassment when I had to get out of the pool earlier than my lighter-skinned cousins or siblings, because along with being darker, I was also always more sensitive. So, I'd sit under a towel, or a blanket, or an umbrella… Pretending it was okay that these labels, which I now know are rooted in anti-blackness and anti-indigeneity, were just thrown on me as if I asked for them. The words were internalized and every syllable was heavy for my little brown body to carry.

The message was sent in all forms of media, also. Little brown girls who looked like me, belonged in the shadows of umbrellas. The shadows kept us hidden from the sun and the light. This didn't only stop us from becoming darker, but it also stopped us from being seen. That feeling echoed inside, for me.

It took years to be proud of my skin. I'm 31 years old. The media still sends those messages, the people still make those comments. Every once in a while it will sting when I hear someone comment on how dark I am getting or get a nickname because of my skin tone. However, I want to acknowledge all of the work I've done to be where I am today. It is because of the knowledge of self-worth, love and acceptance I've built that I can say it sometimes stings, but doesn't penetrate the same as it once did.

I've always been brown, but today, I know the worth that holds.

C/S
(Written March 2019)

I feel a certain type of way when I see a hipster
in Cortez'.
Call me a hater but I don't like when I see a
brand new chola. All of a sudden…
Don't even get me started…

Oh look, I started.

16 year old me comes out wanting to chunk 'em
when I see #ThugLife. I'm stuck between not
"glorifying the gang lifestyle" but knowing
where I'm from. Wearing my cloth belt and
cortez' had me labeled ghetto by half of y'all.

"One's trash is another's treasure", but you can't
pick through my treasure when I never called it
trash.

I wore these shoes knowing if someone
questioned me about them… I stood my ground
or had them snatched.
In no way was I the hardest chola, but I knew to
never back down… because my mom who I
thought was the hardest chola, was finna whoop

my brown ass if I came home barefoot, believe
that. I was so proud when my mom helped me
knot my first chola bands.

My cousin Selena taught me how to do eyeliner
and I thought I was a real badass. I learned that
you can't run from the cops through that big
field in Meadowfair wearing Godfathers because
you will get caught…

I also learned you can't run from the cops in
Cortez' with a worn out grip and I have a scar to
remind me. I couldn't walk with more than 4
friends at a time or we were considered a gang.
You new cholas probably ain't ever had a
Maryjane snap on the way to the party and check
if the bus driver had a safety pin cause you
weren't gonna miss that party! Don't even have
me go in on the godfathers that started talking
after a while… Super glue only goes so far, but I
don't know when I'm going to San Jose Blue
Jeans so this is gonna work. Baby hairs slicked
down. I only used aqua net or rave with the teal
top. I see those of you who asked how I function
with these long ass nails, must have figured it
out since Instagram says it's cool now. I hate
y'all sometimes I really do… What would you
say if someone asked you about your fit though?
I'm just curious… Because all jokes aside, my
boy Ricky never had the chance to answer
before he got shot. Rest in peace to him and my

brother Kane who also was lost in an act of street violence. Those little ghetto boys right? Little hoodlums like me. You see how that works? You see my pain can't be appropriated like my hoops can. Those rosarios and mal de ojos meant the world when my grandma gifted them to me. I don't care how overpriced they were when you paid for them at Urban Outfitters. You can #Chicana all day, but you and I both know you ain't about it. Not that movement, not that life, not no hands. In a couple years you'll find another meaningful piece of culture to take pictures in. And I'll be here, being ghetto. Still. Con safos.

Radical
(Written April 2017)

In a time where we fight to be treated fairly, like our ancestors didn't put in work to pave the way of the footsteps we follow in, we're called extreme. I'm left in awe, as I'm asked, "Don't you think you're being a little too radical?" When SB1070 says it's okay to stop me 'cause I'm brown in Arizona, who questioned the extreme then? When my fellow sisters are frequently missing in Juarez and no action is placed to find them, is that not extreme enough to question? When my brothers are stopped and harassed by the police, they are supposed to be quiet and choose wording correctly to avoid being detained in a land where we have the right to freedom of speech... While on the topic of freedom of speech, let us not forget, it was only 49 years ago we fought to be able to speak Spanish in our classrooms. A language that was forced on us by the same people who then attempted to prohibit it. Sike, think again. We're not allowing you to call shots anymore. This "too extreme" title is still placed on me, instead of the society who tries to oppress me. It's placed on me, amongst other titles. The title that comes with voicing the mistreatment of my people is "too extreme". When I get upset and show it, "I'm emotional". In my protest, "I'm dramatic". When I wear my nameplate necklace, eyeliner and dark lipstick, I'm a chola. God forbid, I protest while I wear my makeup and hoops because I'll be labeled as a hoodlum. Similar to my brother not being able to wear whatever he wants because he'd be "too thug". Let's not forget, we're brown, so of course we're illegal. Somehow, automatically, even though the closest I've ever been to Mexico is San Diego... Unless, you count the fact that wait a second... I'm standing on stolen land in the first place so who's really "illegal" here, baboso? I am native, I am indigenous, me nor any other human is "illegal". I have the weight of the world on my shoulders, as do you my fellow Brown Berets. When we fight our fight and we stand our ground, as this nation tries to hush us with titles that people are too nervous to bear, I'll take it. Call me radical. Call me dramatic. Because drastic times call for drastic measures and we have the blood of warriors running through our veins. We wear it everyday, in our names, in our skin tones. So, if you wanna battle... Let's do this. Our people were built for it and no matter how hard people try to hide that or make us forget it. Don't worry, that's why we're here... To remind them, to strengthen them, to show our history that has been attempted to be erased... And if radical makes you nervous, it should, because it means change. We mean change. So, call us what you want. Just know we'll be ready to take and make anything you call us and own it, as proudly as I brand myself CHICANA. Words don't mean a thing, but our actions, they'll mean everything. No washed-up stereotype name will stop our actions, not an orange-faced sorry excuse for a presidente, AND FOR DAMN SURE, not a wall. Nothing. We're called a movement and we are, but we're also a lifestyle. So, watch us work and work hard, like our ancestors, like our laborers and field workers. Our people are strong. Our strength is our power. We are a powerhouse and we ain't going anywhere. Now, I ask you, why aren't you more extreme? Maybe your question should be redirected. My answer is simple. Por que si se puede.

La Pachuca
(Written June 2021)

Pachuca style was one of the most iconic styles, especially throughout Chicano culture.

In a time when femininity had a few options to choose from and lots of input from society, Pachucas chose to go big and go bad.

They took it upon themselves to encapsulate their beauty and accentuate their womanhood, all while embracing a masculine twist.

La mera meras of their time, they showcased their outfits, make up and hair with no shame and all pride.

Just like their ancestors adorned war paint on their faces, they painted their lips deep browns and reds.

La pachuca is always willing and ready to take on whatever the streets may have brought when they walked outside their doors, including violence and hatred.

Through The Pipeline
(Written December 2023)

I see you, in all your beauty, internal and
external.
I see the weight of what you've carried in your
eyes.
I feel it when you tell your stories so
passionately.
As the memories flow as strong as powerful
waters and high flames
I see the similarity because we and the elements
are feared the same.
More accepted when we're quiet, demonized
when the impact of human evil shows.
We are fire, we are water, and still strong when
looked at as unruly.
We are brown excellence, just as those before us.

So, I ask you to hold your head high as you
consider to walk into the institution this time.
The world isn't set up for us to be honored.
Honor yourself.
This place wasn't meant for us and we know
that. Yet, here we are.
When others were sent to school to succeed,

some were sent because savages should be
funneled in and then out.
From one institution to another is best practice.
School. Foster Care. Prison.
Bad Student, Unwanted Kid, Inhumane Inmate.
Student ID, Jurisdiction Number. Booking
Number. PFN.
All labels. All numbers.
Take their freedom, take their families, take their
name.
Break them. Because if broken enough, how can
one grow?
Break the spirit first, then break the family and
when all else fails break their bodies, right?
Who can come back from that, they've asked.
We will. That's who. Every time. For all of us.
For those gunned down by planted hate, for
those stolen lives from fake protectors.
For those who went missing and the world chose
to look away.
For those who didn't make it through the desert
nights.
For those who left because the silence echoed
too loud in their isolated box.
We will come in the masses for all those who
could no longer.
We are brown excellence, just as those before us.

So, I ask you to hold your head high as you
actively chose to walk into the institution this
time.
You are so far from where you've been, even
though you feel the same sometimes.
Even though you feel stagnant, your internal
growth is there.
Stand in that and accept that others will question
it, that's fine.
As long as you don't allow their uncertainty in
you to impact you questioning yourself.
Anything meant for you is already yours, what
isn't meant for you won't serve you.
We are brown excellence, just as those before us.

So, I tell you to hold your head high as you are
still choosing to walk into the institution this
time.
Every time they broke you, you've healed thus
far.
You've played this game your whole life, and
the ball's in your court.
Shoot your shot for you. Complete this for you.
Heal for you.
Show up brown. Show up tatted. Show up real.
Show up in all of you and yours.
Anything meant for you is already yours, what
isn't meant for you won't serve you.

You are brown excellence, just as those before
you.
And you've broken through their pipeline.

Manos
(Written February 2024)

Shades of brown manos.
Hands which have held a lifetime of...
Everything.

As the burden falls on our shoulders,
carrying the weight as the eldest daughters
in brown households.

We've used our hands to carry it all...
The food, the babies, the other hands we hold...
The tears we wipe, the clutter we move...
Physical. Mental. Emotional.
We carry it all. We hold it all.

Blessings to curses,
Some ours, some not.
Some chosen, some we inherit.
Love and hurt in each crease.
Joy and pain in each vein.
Laughter and tears in each fold.
Every scar, every wrinkle earned through
experience and time.
My grandma's hand in mine, like my mom
couldn't experience.

Love learned through proven practice...
And not evenly spread through generational
actions.
It looked different each time, but always true
and strong.

Just as our hands, in all their shades of brown.

Baby Love
(Written February 2024)

If you could see yourself through my eyes...
Would your world change?

To see your beauty radiate from your internal
spirit.
To see how gently you love despite you thinking
it's weak.
To see all your potential, in all its glory,
when you're balancing the frustration of your
growing phase.

I admire the relief in your laughter
when we crack up after you finally realized it
was okay to cry...
More than okay actually.
That moment before you pick up your armor
back up, piece by piece,
and place that burden of wanting to cover your
emotions,
back on your shoulders.

I want to remove it for you.
But I shove my selfish thoughts aside,
and force my feet into the dirt from afar,

to watch you grow in your own garden, in your
own way.

I trust you'll continue to grow strong and be
okay on your own.
I remind myself how miraculous you are.

I comfort myself know you to know, as I do,
that sunflowers know to turn towards each other
when the sun isn't shining.
Mi girasol, my baby love,
whether I'm the other sunflower or you find that
light elsewhere,
just know I never doubt you.

I only want to affirm your light.
I want you to know your power.
Then I tell myself, "Cabrona, she knows."
And you do, you always have,
because you can see yourself through my eyes,
but more importantly,
you have your own.

Un Dia A La Vez
(Written January 2024)

Just be happy. Why won't you just be happy?

As if waking up and choosing to not know how
to navigate life is a choice.
As if I get to choose a simple option of today,
not listening to that voice
Or some days its voices, as in multiple, so many
And the days get heavier the longer I'm away
from the Henny
Because I'm trying to choose happiness, I swear
that I am
But this chemical imbalance is taking all that I
have
It's darkening days when I'm struggling to
breathe
It's consuming my mind, leaving me begging for
ease
I don't remember the light, it's been some time
now
It's shifted from second nature to first, behind
the tears of a clown
I'm smiling now but I'm crying inside
Even in moments of joy, it still won't subside

I'm still here

It's overwhelming, I don't want advice
I'm trying to navigate through virtue and vice
Minute by minute, one day at a time
I can't describe it, so I just say I'm fine
I know I'm surrounded, so many around
My mind is a dark room, pitch black no sound

I try to be happy, that's not all it takes

Rationally, I hear you, but shadows cover logic
In a room full of people, I'm lonely
In my mind, I'm trapped
Then one day I'm balanced

& I am still here
Until my mind becomes a prison again

Wander
(Written February 2024)

What do you think about when your mind
wanders?
Is it love? Or avoidance of?

Physically I run.
Mentally I stay.

Caught between experiences, both past and
possible.
'Past' brings pain and residual stains of fear.
Yet, 'possible' brings hope and a yearning to tear
down walls.

I'll allow my heart to wander and wonder if
you'll do the same.
And if you wander towards love or further
towards the side of avoidance.

eNVy
(Written February 2024)

When I see you laugh, it makes me proud.
I think of your laughter and I correlate it to love.
We're so different, yet much the same.

I long for a hug, for it's affirmation of
connection.
Envious when I see it given to others, even
though it makes me happy to see.

It's taken time, but I now know,
difference doesn't mean absence, as your
younger daughter thought.
Because I, your older daughter, know your
humor is your connection.

Humor is laughter.
Laughter is love.
Love is consistency.
Consistency hasn't always been consistent in our
lives.

Yet, you have,
And so has your love.

Love always,
Your daughter in all ways.

Pink Skies
(Written November 2023)

It was an honor and it still is.

To meet her in all her humor, sassiness, light,
And of course, her love.

No longer in physical form, but a spirit as
vibrant as ever.
Her humor shows, as we trip over thin air.
Her vibrant personality will always show as
music plays through our speakers.
Her love will always show when the sun touches
our skin,
in the most perfect way.
It will be affirmed when the breeze near the
beach flows through our hair.

Just as when she was here, in physical form,
She'll continue to always make her presence
known.
Whether it be an unexpected dime you find,
or a single beautiful rose you notice.

That's your girl, turning the skies pink.

Seven Trees
(Written October 2022)

Dedicated to that little brown girl from the South
Side,
who thought better days would never come.

If I could tell myself then that one day we'd be
writing our own stories,
where we stood in truth and power
and weren't broken down by court reports and
violations I would.

I'd let her know we'd change policies one day,
we'd organize within our communities, we'd
shut down jails….
We. Would. Heal.

We'd build our family back together after it was
broken and separated.
We'd help others amplify their voices
and encourage them to be in their power too.

She'd probably mad dog me and walk out the
room, but I'd tell her.

Dedicated to every kid I've ever worked with,

to every kid who has ever felt alone
or done
or felt like they had no sense of agency in their
lives.

You are loved, you are worthy,
you are the epitome of power and you are
sacred.

I'm still proud as can be to be that kid from the
South Side.
That will never change.

We out here. Build on your community.

We are the ones we've been waiting for.

Childhood
(Written September 2022)

Some days it still hits a lil' different….
Some days multiple areas of my life came back
instantly.

At tables with those ears which never listened,
those who had cold eyes and sharp tongues,
rooted in the darkness that targeted my
ancestors,
whom this system was built on.
Family separation is a realm of its own.

Our stories matter and youth voice is often the
most silenced,
on the system side AND the family side.
Let's be real.

Big eyes and tiny feet walking into these big
buildings
as these little brown kids know nothing but
uncertainty
and that overwhelming awareness of no
self-determination in these buildings.

Adults now, and feelings remain for so many
kids who walk into these buildings.
Internally, still youth who try and swallow the
tears,
as you read "JUSTICE" in bold capital letters,
while you feel the opposite in the pit of your
stomach…
I see you.

It can get better, I promise.
We can walk out of the building now,
and though these buildings make us feel like
"inferior" is written on our foreheads at times,
we are not...
No longer scared, lost or confused.

I stand in the power I've always had
and will help others stand in theirs, as well.

Don't let the cold eyes and the sharp tongues
shade your resilience.
We will change the world and our ancestors will
always have our back.

Radiate
(Written August 2017)

Unsolicited comments on how strong feminine energy can be.
Sometimes in a good way, sometimes negatively, depending on the emotions shown at the moment.

When upset or sad, energy radiates off like crazy,
And the same thing when happy or excited.

Can't control when people feed off happiness, and nobody seems to mind.

Nobody has said, "We feed off of your spirit and I want to let you know I appreciate your good energy."...
Of course, neither is it expected.
But when having a bad day, week, whatever it may be...

Maybe you're talking less than normal or you don't open up about feelings...
People get very bothered. So, one is expected often, sometimes even pressured

to openly share why they're less talkative or less
enthusiastic...
And of course, reminded of how strong feminine
energy is.

Despite being reflective of interactions with
people,
and of course, very accountable.
Never has it served one to be guilt-tripped about
my energy.

Can we control how you receive it?
We can't control how we receive yours,
unless it's ill-intended.

No yelling, no cussing, not throwing a fit, nor
putting anyone down...
Energy is simply radiating.
No thanks towards people for their positive
energy that is fed off of,
maybe second guess it before pointing out
when energy is going through some thangs
either.

Feminine energy is strong like every woman's
has been in the bloodline
and as they carry the energy of many of their
ancestors...

There is no on-and-off switch for when it
radiates.

Not apologizing for that anymore.

Remember
(Written November 2017)

Our cultura is beautiful, but it comes with a long
history.
A long unknown history and continued battle for
our survival.

We are the native people to turtle island and,
yet...
We seem to be the most forgotten and
unspoken-about people here...
Let me remind you Thanks-Taking is not a day
about some people
who got lost and brought illness and disease and
lies to my people,
while on the other side of the continent another
invader
was doing the same thing.

This is about indigenous resistance and
indigenous existence.
We are here. Our spiritual practices are here.
We are alive, and though this country that was
built on our resources and our backs
makes it extremely hard, we will continue to live
and thrive.

We talk about native genocide as if it were a
thing of the past...
We speak about it as if it has ended. This is
ongoing.
This continues. This is strategic...

You are on native land right NOW.
San Jose is occupied Muwekma Ohlone
ancestral homeland,
and their descendants are still proudly here,
very connected to their traditions and history,
but due to indigenous erasure, few know this.

Year 2016, 5,712 known incidents of missing
and murdered indigenous women.
Only 116 of those were logged into the DOJ
database.
Across the country, indigenous women are 10x
more likely
to be killed than the national average murder
rate.

As you package and sell our culture like it's a
hot commodity,
remember the fate that continues to be directed
at those who hold these traditions and medicine
so sacred for many generations.

Those that will continue to protect the sacred,

hold healing space and continue traditions long
after a fad is over.

Women are sacred.
Dedicated to all of our missing sisters.
You are not forgotten.
Your families are not alone.
You are loved.
Your fight is not over.
We will continue to push...

For awareness, for policy change,
for healing, for proper burials,
for actual investigations,
for answers and
for the dignity and justice you deserve.

You are worthy of that and so much more.

Ometeotl.

www.ingramcontent.com/pod-product-compliance
Lightning Source LLC
Chambersburg PA
CBHW061726130726
47996CB00006B/2525